1/02

Everything You Need to Know About

Wicca

Wicca is a religion centered on nature and rooted in ancient pagan beliefs.

Everything You Need to Know About

Wicca

Geraldine Giordano

The Rosen Publishing Group, Inc.
New York

This book is dedicated to Wiccans everywhere.

Published in 2001 by The Rosen Publishing Group, Inc.
29 East 21st Street, New York, NY 10010

Library of Congress Cataloging-in-Publication Data

Giordano, Geraldine.
    Everything you need to know about Wicca / by Geraldine Giordano. — 1st ed.
    p. cm. — (The need to know library)
Includes bibliographical references and index.
ISBN 0-8239-3401-2
1. Witchcraft—Juvenile literature. [1. Witchcraft.] I. Title. II. Series.
BF1566 .G56 2001
299—dc21

                                     00-010929

Manufactured in the United States of America

Contents

Introduction

When you hear the word "witchcraft," what do you think of? Do you picture women dressed in black flying on broomsticks? Or maybe you envision a scene from *The Wizard of Oz* or *The Craft*?

Wicca is a form of witchcraft. It is believed to be derived from what is known as the "Old Religion." Wicca is a religion of nature. Its holidays fall on each solstice (the two days of the year when the sun is furthest from the equator) and each equinox (the two days of the year when the sun crosses the equator and day and night are of equal length). The phases of the moon are held in great importance by Wiccans. During these phases, members gather in covens and practice their beliefs through the performance of rituals.

In this book, you will learn about Wicca—the myths that have developed around it, its history, and its practices. The information in this book is a collection of what many Wiccans believe and practice, but since there are many branches of Wicca, the contents of this book should be considered only one version.

Most of what is known about Wicca comes from paganism, which developed thousands of years ago. Paganism is the term for the mixture of many spiritual belief systems that are nature-based. Pagans believe that the entity they worship is both male and female. Wicca is believed to be a modernized version of paganism. Because of this, Wicca is described as "neo-pagan."

The practice of Wicca is growing all around the world. There are many new books about Wicca that can be found in bookstores and libraries. What used to be a secret way of life is slowly coming out in the open. Not only that, but more Wiccans are beginning to call themselves "witches." What was once considered to be a derogatory and demeaning term is also changing with the times.

Ancient figures and artwork suggest that people were worshipping spirits of nature as long as 40,000 years ago.

Chapter One

What Is Wicca?

Ancient people believed that the earth gave life to plants, animals, and people through fire, water, air, and earth. Figures in the form of woman, and woman with child, date back to 40,000 to 10,000 BC. It is therefore believed that the people of that time worshiped a spirit known as Goddess of the earth or Mother Goddess. This female figure is strongly identified with Wicca.

Paganism

Paganism is a set of beliefs based on a mixture of different faiths. It is believed to have been the first nature-based religion. Pagans felt that people should be one with the earth. They created gods and goddesses who represented events that occurred in their lives, elements of nature, and seasons. As time passed, societies were worshiping thousands of gods and goddesses, each representing different aspects of nature. Rituals were developed that fell around solstices and equinoxes because of their importance to the cycle of seasons and living things.

The Shamans

It is believed that shamanism was the first religion. It was a religion that Native Americans practiced thousands of years ago. The people who practiced the rituals of shamanism were referred to as shamans. According to shamanism, spirits and other dimensions of reality exist that are beyond what can be seen, heard, smelled, tasted, or touched. Shamans reached this plane by practicing rituals. First, they left the physical plane. Some of the ways they did this included fasting, meditating, and taking substances that would cause them to hallucinate. They also wounded themselves with knives, because bleeding caused them to become weak and hallucinate. While in a trance or other realm, the shamans were able to learn about other dimensions. People established ceremonies based on what the shamans learned. These ceremonies became daily practice. Some of the later methods of conducting rituals included the use of objects such as drums, rattles, music, chants, and dancing. The practice was considered spiritual and became a religion. Aspects of Wicca were taken from these rites and rituals.

Churches such as this were built on the same grounds that had been used as pagan places of worship.

Christianity, the New Religion

When the religion of Christianity came into being, pagans were drawn to it. The first reason for this was that Christianity allowed pagans to practice a structured system of beliefs with fewer complications than were found in Judaism, which was a prominent religion of the time. Also, the rituals that Jesus performed were considered mysteries and even miracles, and this was appealing to pagans as well. A final reason pagans were drawn to Christianity was because it promised a life after death. This gave hope to people who weren't happy with this life and who could live knowing that there was something better to come. Many pagans happily converted to this "new" religion. Churches were built on the same grounds that had been used as pagan places of worship. The Christian holidays were observed around the same times as those that the pagans celebrated.

Kings asked their subjects to convert because they thought that Jesus would aid them in battle. Once kings started to successfully win battles, they believed it was Jesus who made it happen for them. It soon became required that everyone practice Christianity. This started as an innocent request, but eventually turned into a life-threatening situation.

The Burning Times

In the 1560s, it was decided that people must convert to Christianity or die. Those who wanted to practice a religion other than Christianity were forced to do so in secret. Witch-hunts were created to find people who took part in this secret practice. Committees were formed to conduct the hunts. Thus began the "Burning Times."

The majority of the victims during the Burning Times were women. There are various reasons for this. Women were believed to be weak and vulnerable to evil forces; they would easily make pacts with the devil. It was also believed that women had affairs with the devil. The focus of the blame was put on the "strange" people of a village who were usually widowed women or midwives. It was believed that they used evil powers to create curses, illness, and even death.

During the sixteenth century, those believed to be witches were killed.

Because the people who were responsible for "saving" a village from the horrible "witches" were considered heroic, witch-hunting became a highly profitable occupation. An instruction manual was created to aid the witch-hunters called the *Malleus Maleficarum*. In the book, people were told a witch cannot bleed. Using a retractable poker, an accused witch was stabbed at and if she didn't bleed, she was sentenced to a trial.

The Trial and Sentencing

The women who were sent to trial were usually killed. They were tortured and forced to confess to the accusations. Wives, mothers, and sisters were all accused and nothing could be done to stop it. If someone tried to contest the accusation, he or she ran the risk of being put on trial as well. Once the accused confessed, they were executed. Witches were always executed in public, primarily by hanging, stoning, or burning at a stake in the center of town. Before this was done, a "witch" was usually whipped, slashed, and cut. It is estimated that between the years 1570 and 1760, 100,000 women were killed. But other estimates say that throughout Europe, 3 to 10 million women were killed. To Wiccans today, the Burning Times are considered a women's holocaust.

Wicca

Wicca is a religion of nature that has its origins in pagan beliefs. It is a modern religion that is open to change and personalization. Its followers celebrate the changes of the seasons and the phases of the moon. It is said to have been "created" by Gerald Gardner in the early twentieth century. He wrote books based on the information he learned in his coven. His books were the first of their kind about witchcraft. The first people to practice Wicca called themselves "Gardnerians." Because of this, Gardner is referred to as the father of modern paganism.

Wiccans believe that there is a higher being or greater power that is both male and female. The male aspect is known as the God, and the female aspect is called the Goddess. The reason that both a male and female figure are worshiped at once is quite simple. It gives balance to everything. And balance is equality. As viewed by Wicca philosophy, if God is only male, then why would He have bothered to create a female? If He is in everything, then He must have feminine characteristics as well. This higher being is responsible for the creation of the universe and exists in everything it has created: the sun, the moon, the earth, plants, trees, oceans, animals, and us.

The Wiccan Rede

Wiccans firmly believe in what they call the "Wiccan Rede," or three-fold law. They believe that whatever people do will return to them times three during their lifetimes. As a result of their beliefs, there is no Satan or hell-like place in Wicca. They don't believe that they will be punished in an afterlife for their wrong-doings; Wiccans believe that wrongdoing will come back to them through karma. Karma is the energy created from every thought, emotion, and action. If people do something wrong to someone, that bad energy is going to come back to them in the future. For example, if they steal from someone, something will be stolen from them.

You may ask yourself: If they don't believe in hell, do Wiccans also not believe in heaven? Wiccans believe in reincarnation. Death is not final. To most Wiccans, death is part of a cycle. This cycle is defined as birth/death/rebirth. The closest thing to heaven in Wiccan philosophy is Summerlands. This is the place where a person's soul goes to rest before it's ready to start its next life. In the Summerlands, people get the opportunity to reunite with their loved ones.

Wiccans also respect that everyone has free will. They believe that nothing should be done to another if he or she objects. This is expressed in a rhyme that most Wiccans know and follow. It says, "Eight words the Wiccan Rede fulfill: As it harm none, do what you will."

Wiccans extend the idea of free will to all people, including those who do not practice Wicca. They do not believe that Wiccans should force others to join their religion. They do not think that their system is the only system people should practice. Wiccans respect the fact that other religions exist. They only encourage others to choose the path with which they feel most comfortable.

The Deities

In Wicca, the universal force is composed of two parts or halves—male and female, or the God and the Goddess. From this division, all entities within the universe— humans, plants, and animals—are then further divided by gender. Some Wiccans name their deities using names from older religions or Greek mythology. This naming is a way of personifying what each deity symbolizes and helps others understand what they represent.

The God

The God represents the masculine side of the universal force. He is the hunter and protector of the forests and its creatures. He represents sexuality and good, and is the compassionate father to all. According to paganism, the God is described as a horned man. It is believed that ancient people created his image in this way because the animals they hunted had horns. They chose to depict their god this way so that he would bring them success in hunting.

The God's symbol is the sun. Both the God and the sun represent life, strength, protection, and creation. Like

The Many Faces of the God

The God is often personified with a name and an image. For example, Greeks referred to their male deity as Pan. Pan was half-man and half-god. He was called upon to make the land fertile and to help with the flocks.

In England, the God is known as the Green Man or "Jack-in-the-Green." The Green Man often has horns and wears a mask of oak leaves. He represents all of the spirits in the forest's trees and plants. He is responsible for bringing rain in order to create life.

Romans and Celts worshiped Cernunnos, the male horned god. His image is a man with serpent legs and the head of a bull. Like the Wiccan god, he represented fertility and rules the hunt.

the sun, the God rules the day. His counterpart, the Goddess, is symbolized by the moon and rules the night.

The God has a life cycle. He is born at the winter solstice, unites with the Goddess in the spring and dies at the summer solstice. The major events that happen in His life fall around Wiccan holidays.

When Christianity was created and made the required religion, the Christians used the Wiccan god as a means to steer people away from paganism and other local religious beliefs. By creating "Satan" in the image of a horned man that looked much like the Wiccan god, many began to believe that those who worshiped Him were devil-worshippers.

This misconception is true even today. Many mistake Wiccans for Satanists. They assume that the Wiccan horned god is Satan. This is disappointing to Wiccans because they consider their god a peaceful, loving father who protects them. He is gentle and good.

The Goddess

The Goddess is the female aspect of the universal force. She is known as the Great Mother, and is a symbol of fertility because she creates life. She is also the destroyer because she knows that the life she creates will eventually die. She shows herself in emotions, intuitions, and the power to heal. The moon is her symbol.

It is believed that in ancient times the Goddess was the first to be worshiped. Fertility of the land was of great importance to the ancients who grew crops.

The Many Faces of the Goddess

Like the God, the Goddess was given different personifications in different cultures. The Goddess has three stages of life: the maiden, the mother, and the crone. This is referred to as the "Goddess trinity." These life stages each correspond to phases of the moon. The maiden represents the waxing moon, the mother, the full moon, and the crone, the waning moon. There is also a dark side to the Goddess. She is ruler of the underworld where one goes after death to face judgment. It is also a place of rest for the bodyless soul.

The Greek goddess Artemis, known to the Romans as Diana, was considered the maiden within the Goddess trinity. As the goddess of the hunt, she represented power. The statue on the right is of Diana of Ephesus. Selene, the mother within the trinity, was the Greek goddess who ruled the moon. She is depicted as a woman in a chariot, flying through the night.

The crone of the trinity is Hecate, ruler of the moon's dark side. She destroyed life and was responsible for nightmares. She was portrayed as a woman with three heads, to represent facing life's crossroads.

ARTEMIS

Anthropologists believe that these people thought the Goddess had created herself and everything else. Some of the earliest drawings and statues found of the Goddess date back as far as 35,000 BC. A famous carving found in France dating back to 19,000 BC, called the Venus of Laussel, depicts a woman holding a bison horn in one hand.

Branches of Wicca

There are many branches of Wicca. Each has kept the core system of beliefs but focuses on different aspects. The following are some examples of branches of Wicca:

- Alexandrian Wicca. This branch was founded in England in the 1960s by Alex and Maxine Sanders. This branch is similar to the one started by Gerald Gardner except that it is not as strict. Its followers were among the first to allow clothing to be worn during ritual's.

- Celtic Wicca. This branch uses traditional beliefs along with the incorporation of Celtic gods and goddesses, spiritualism, and faery magic.

- Dianic Wicca. Dianic Wicca is a feminist path that worships the goddess Diana.

- Family Traditions. This branch is practiced by Wiccan families who worship in secret. Over

This is a kitchen witch grinding herbs in a bowl. Kitchen witches often focus on practical magic and natural remedies.

the years, their traditions have been passed down from generation to generation.

- Kitchen Wicca or Kitchen Witch. This branch focuses on practical beliefs of Wicca and its practical magic. Its followers use everyday items to practice their beliefs. Many live in urban areas.

- Shamanic Wicca. This tradition concentrates on connecting with the spirit world. Much of their worship is focused on healing.

- Strega Wicca. This is an Italian branch of Wicca that is believed to have started in the thirteenth century. This branch follows the teachings of Aradia, daughter of Diana. It is believed that Aradia brought witches to the earth.

21

Chapter Two | Hollywood Stereotypes and Other Myths

Stereotypes about witches have been around since the beginning of time. During the Burning Times, "witches" were even murdered because of them. Throughout the years, Wiccans have had to withstand the criticism and judgment of many individuals and groups. Hollywood, in particular, has portrayed the witch in a number of misleading ways.

Green Face, Warts, and—Oh My!

Who can forget the Wicked Witch of the West in *The Wizard of Oz*? She was lean, mean, and green. With the tip of her finger, she could have made the Scarecrow burst into flames. Throughout the history of television, witches have been stereotyped as evil, wicked women who want to hurt or curse good people. Where did this image come from? There are several theories.

In the Burning Times, witch-hunters captured women accused of being witches. These women had to

The Wicked Witch of the West from *The Wizard of Oz* is one of the most enduring popular images of witches.

endure much torture. They were beaten, poked with hot pokers, had their limbs pulled, and their hair torn out. As a result, their faces often became greenish from bruises. Their noses were broken and left crooked. Cuts and sores caused by poking made them look as if they had warts on their faces. Their bodies were pulled and beaten which caused them to hunch over or otherwise look deformed. Besides the torture, these women were starved and dehydrated.

This may be how the image of a witch came about. If a woman who endured this torture walked down the street, you would describe her as a hunchback with a crooked nose, green and bruised skin, straggly hair, and warts and lesions on her face. Does this image sound familiar to you? Many images of witches, whether they appear in movies or are drawn as cartoon characters, look just like this.

Satan

How does Satan figure into Wicca? He doesn't, really. Wiccans do not believe in an evil being named Satan. In Wicca, one is responsible for his or her actions. If one chooses to perform evil, he or she does so willingly. The devil is not responsible.

However, when Christianity came into being, it linked the idea of a devil or evil being to paganism, by making the devil a horned creature that looked like the pagan god Pan. People who wanted to practice paganism instead of converting to Christianity were accused of being devil-worshippers when they were really only worshiping their own god of nature.

Magick

Magick is a spiritual practice that uses energy generated through ritual to create a desired change. To do this, a spell has to be cast. By concentrating on an object—such as a lit candle—Wiccans are able to focus on a problem, concern, or wish and create change. This concentration creates a positive energy force and then the request can be made. The idea is very similar to prayer.

There are many different types of magick, each named by the object that is the focus of the ritual. Some

Hollywood movies often portray stereo-types of witches. In this scene from *Practical Magic*, witches are shown casting spells by using whipped cream.

examples are candle magick, knot magick, and runic magick. These types of magick all use the same principles, but different objects to create energy. Magick however, is not supernatural, as it is often portrayed in many books, movies, and television shows. You can find many examples in Hollywood. For instance, in the movie *Practical Magic*, there is a scene in which Sandra Bullock's character is reading her morning paper. As she reads, a spoon is stirring her cup of coffee by itself. In the television sitcom *Sabrina the Teenage Witch*, Sabrina and her aunts can appear and disappear in other worlds and places. They can also drink potions that alter their physical appearance or freeze time.

These are some of the misconceptions about witches and Wicca. Some have been drawn from silly myths or pop culture. Others have arisen from misleading stereo-types that have formed over many years. In all, they have caused much negativity and violence against Wiccans.

Chapter Three

Aspects of Wicca

Wiccans come to Wicca by numerous routes. Some become interested in certain tools of divination such as tarot cards or runes. Others discover books that give them a better understanding of the topic. Still others discover Wicca through a friend.

Once you choose to follow the path of Wicca, you have to do a lot of research. Many choose to conduct the research on their own. They discover that Wiccans tend to fall into two different categories—those who practice alone (solitary practitioners) and those who practice in a group or coven.

Covens

A coven is a group of Wiccans who have many common beliefs. When they gather together, they are led by a high priestess and/or a high priest. The high priestess represents the Goddess. The high priest represents the God.

Some people who practice Wicca prefer to perform their rituals within a coven.

Not all covens are run by both. Some are led by one or the other. The high priest or priestess is considered a teacher. He or she decides what the group is going to learn during a meeting. The high priest or priestess also leads rituals that the coven performs. He or she is a lot like a priest in a church or a rabbi in a synagogue.

Another job that the high priest or priestess does is arrange seminars and workshops for his or her group to attend. These events can be something as simple as a reading or as fancy as a festival. Sometimes, the workshop will fall on a Wiccan holiday. How the coven is run is also determined by the high priest or priestess. This means he or she can choose to have the group follow tradition or base the group's activities on his or her own system of beliefs. (There must, however, be some agreement by the members of the coven about what is being taught.)

Initiation

In some covens, Wiccans graduate once they reach a certain level of learning. This is their initiation day after which they can officially be called "witch." Not only do witches have to know the lessons that they have been taught, they also have to be able to perform some aspect of Wicca. From there, witches can continue their education until they reach the status of high priest or priestess.

Solitary Practice

Some people choose to practice Wicca alone. These Wiccans are called solitary practitioners or solitary Wiccans. Some prefer to be alone so that the opinions of others won't stand in their way. Some people are just naturally private. They consider Wicca to be their religion and like the idea of performing rituals by themselves. Some Wiccans start out as solitary and then join a coven. They feel they should have some education before finding others. Others remain solitary because they can't find a coven or can't find other witches to unite with to form a coven. Sometimes, witches will find a coven but then feel that the group's interests are different from their own. These are just some of the reasons people choose to be solitary.

Solitary Wiccans study just like those who are members of a coven. They read books, attend workshops, and perform rituals. In most cases, they will set up an altar in their home.

Solitary Initiation

Solitary practitioners usually set their own goals. They decide what they are required to learn. Once they have met their goals, they are ready to initiate themselves. This is done by performing a "self-dedication." This means that they are dedicating themselves to the God and Goddess. This ceremony is private and done outdoors.

Which Way Should I Go?

If you are interested in practicing Wicca yourself, you may wonder how you should start. After reading about solitary Wiccans and those who are part of a coven, you may also wonder how to go about choosing which path you should follow. It all depends on you. Here are some questions you can ask yourself to help you make your decision. If you answer yes to the following questions, the solitary path may be your best choice.

- Am I a strong, independent person?

- Do I want to study at my own pace?

- Will I want to practice privately?

- Would I have a hard time compromising some of my beliefs to be part of a group?

If you answer yes to the questions below, choosing to join a coven may be best for you.

- Do I need a teacher to help me along?

- Do I like working with others in large groups?

- Am I able to get along with others?

- Can I compromise when I don't agree with someone else's opinion?

Once you decide that you seriously want to pursue Wicca, you must organize your thoughts and beliefs. Why do you want to become a witch? How will this religion benefit your life?

This choice must feel right in your heart. This choice is a spiritual change, a realization that your current system of beliefs does not fit into your lifestyle, or does not fit in with the person you are becoming.

Upon reading about Wicca, you may decide that there are some aspects of it that you would prefer not to incorporate into your system of beliefs. This is completely normal. You are not required to follow a set of rules that are set in stone. Wicca can be personalized to fit your lifestyle and your beliefs. You should only do what makes you feel comfortable.

Chapter Four

Sabbats: Wiccan Holidays

Wiccans have their own holidays, which are known as sabbats. They are celebrated throughout the year and correspond with the stories of the God and Goddess.

Yule

The story begins with the Goddess giving birth to the God. This happens around December 21, a day known as Yule, which means "wheel" in the Old Norse language. Since this is also the start of winter—the winter solstice—Wiccans take the opportunity to celebrate the birth and forget about the dreariness of winter.

To celebrate Yule, Wiccans decorate a tree with appropriate symbols and other ornaments. These decorations are almost always handmade, using natural materials. For example, garlands for the tree can be made from strings of popcorn or flowers. And ornaments can include fruits such as apples, oranges, and lemons. Some Wiccans even hang crystals on their trees.

Along with the custom of decorating a tree, Wiccans may choose to light an oak or pine Yule log. Symbols and drawings of the God are often carved onto the log. These drawings symbolize His birth. The ashes of the log are later spread throughout gardens to bring fertility to the land and ensure that the crops will be prosperous.

Imbolc

The next sabbat is called Imbolc and falls on February 2. By this day, the Goddess has recovered from giving birth to the God. She is still weak, but her health is slowly being restored. The days are beginning to get longer, which means there will be more daylight. The growing strength of the Goddess is symbolized by this increase in daylight. Brightly colored candles are usually lit to honor the sun and the coming light. Wiccans eat spicy and hot foods that contain peppers, onions, garlic, and chives. Spicy foods and herbs are symbolic of the sun.

Ostara

Ostara is celebrated on March 21. Winter is officially over and spring has begun. Fire and water combine and fertilize the earth so that new growth can occur. Wiccans celebrate by decorating hard-boiled eggs that symbolize the rebirth that spring is going to bring; some have an egg hunt. The eggs are hidden before a ritual and then

These Wiccans are celebrating the fall festival of Mabon.

hunted for. Tradition says that for every egg you find, a wish will be granted to you at Beltane (the next holiday). Ostara can be considered a Wiccan Mother's Day. Mothers and daughters bond to signify the physical connection that has been made between them.

Beltane

On April 30, Wiccans celebrate Beltane, which is also known as May Day. Beltane symbolizes the union of the God and Goddess. Wiccans ceremonially plant seeds as an offering to the Goddess and spirits associated with the earth. A maypole is the main focus of the celebration. It represents the God, who is the male fertility symbol. Wiccans gather around the pole and decorate it with flowers, long strands of ribbon, and herbs, and then dance around it. As they dance around the pole, the ribbons become intertwined with one another, like a braid or weave. This process of taking two pieces and uniting them is a symbol of the God and Goddess's union.

Some Wiccans celebrate this day in a park or forest, and tie strips of cloth to nearby trees and bushes. These decorations are offerings to the spirits of the area. If the spirits are drawn to these gifts, then special favors and wishes will be granted to the ones who marked them.

Midsummer

Midsummer happens on June 21, the longest day of the year. The sun is at its strongest on this day, so midsummer is considered a magical day. This is the best time to perform rituals that have to do with love, friendship, and healing. Wiccans celebrate by wearing garlands made from freshly picked herbs, and by eating fresh fruits of all kinds. They take special care to acknowledge that this day represents the power of life.

Lughnusadh

Lughnusadh (usually referred to as Lamas) falls on August 1, the day of the first harvest of the year. It celebrates the success of the crops that were planted in the spring. An old custom is to have a fair or market around this time.

Mabon

Mabon is the sabbat that falls on September 21. It represents the completion of the harvest that began at Lughanshan. At this time, the leaves fall from the trees and the crops have stopped growing, and the God is preparing for his rest and death.

Samhain

Samhain (pronounced SO-en) falls on October 31 and is also known as Halloween, Feast of the Dead, or All Hallow's Eve. Samhain is Irish for "end of summer." It marks the beginning of winter and it is at this time that the last of the crops are picked. According to the story of the God and Goddess, this is when the God dies. However, this is not a sad time because Wiccans know that His rebirth is going to come.

It is believed that at Samhain, communication with the dead is possible, because the living and dead share the same space on the earth on that day. It is a time to remember friends and loved ones who have passed. On this day, Wiccans reflect on life and remember that everyone will experience one common event—death.

These primary Wiccan holidays are important times of the year during which Wiccans honor the God and the Goddess and draw strength from the universe. During these holidays, Wiccans gather together, eat, drink, perform rituals, and celebrate the cycles of life and nature.

Wiccans perform rituals during sabbats and other special occasions.

Chapter Five

Wiccan Rituals

A ritual is something Wiccans perform to get a desired result. For instance, they may perform a ritual for healing, protection, or love. The ritual is where magick comes into play. Many people are drawn to this aspect of Wicca. Rituals are performed during sabbats, different phases of the moon, and other special occasions. A ritual can be as simple as meditating and giving thanks or it can be complicated, involving a lot of people and a variety of objects.

What on Earth Are They Doing?

Cassie lives by a park. One night, during a full moon, when she glanced out of her window, something caught her eye. She looked closer and saw some flickering lights. Cassie realized the lights were candles that people were holding. She watched as the people walked clockwise in a circle, making hand gestures. Then the people started to dance.

Cassie wondered what these people were doing. She thought that they could be witches. She knew some people who were part of a coven. She knew they met and performed ceremonies. In fact, there was a girl in one of Cassie's classes who talked about Wicca. The girl, Jessica, had told Cassie and her friends about circle meetings she had attended. "I can't wait to get to school tomorrow to tell Jessica about this and ask her about her circle meetings," Cassie thought as she reluctantly went back to her homework.

To start a ritual, Wiccans will state a purpose. What do they want to accomplish? Are they interested in healing themselves or someone else? Is there something they want to learn? Is it going to be done to celebrate an event or occasion? Once this is decided, they choose a time for the ritual to take place.

The Elements

Wiccans believe there are four elements that, combined, make up and sustain life. They are air, fire, water, and earth. These four elements are considered the building blocks of all earthly creations. Everything you see, touch, hear, and feel is made up of at least one of these elements. In addition, each element is aligned with a direction—east, west, north, or south. The four directions are referred to as the four corners.

A Wiccan altar is arranged with objects that represent the four elements—air, fire, water, and earth.

When Wiccans gather in a circle, they call upon the four corners. When they do this, they are calling each element to the circle. Air is located to the east. Fire is located to the south. Water is located to the west, and earth is located to the north. This is done for protection. Each element is present to watch over the coven and help ensure that the desired changes are made. These four elements also have individual characteristics and are called on for different results in rituals.

Air

Air is the element of intelligence, inspiration, and imagination. It rules your ideas, dreams, and wishes. Wiccans use the element of air or objects that symbolize this element when they are searching for something that is lost, are in need of instruction (from the higher power), and when they want to visualize a desired result. Air is an element of the God.

Fire

Fire is the element of passion, creativity, willpower, and sensuality. It represents the physical and spiritual aspects of sexuality. Wiccans use the element of fire when they want to heal someone, make something pure, or spark someone's creativity. Fire rules every aspect of candle magick and is another element of the God.

Water

Water is the element of emotion and intuition. It represents love, compassion, and family. Wiccans use the element of water when they want to cast spells and perform rituals of love, friendship, happiness, and fertility. Water rules psychic ability and spells that involve mirrors. Water is an element of the Goddess.

Earth

Earth is the element of the physical body and endurance. It represents wisdom, strength, growth, and prosperity. Wiccans use the element of earth for spells and rituals involving business matters, financial prosperity, and stability. Earth rules knot magick and is also an element of the Goddess.

The Moon and Its Phases

The moon has a monthly cycle that it completes about every twenty-eight-and-a-half days. A new moon,

which is when the moon is completely dark, begins the cycle. As the moon rotates around the earth, it moves through different phases. A waxing moon describes the moon on its way to becoming full. The full moon phase (the phase you are probably most familiar with) is the time at which you can see the moon in its entirety. The final phase, a waning moon, is the time in which the moon moves from full back to new. Different phases of the moon are used for different types of rituals.

- When the moon is waxing (on its way to becoming full), it is the time to perform a ritual to begin something new.

- When the moon is full, this is a time for transformation because it's at its most powerful. This is because the moon is complete and strong. Wiccans use the night of a full moon to celebrate the presence of the Goddess on the earth.

- When the moon is waning (on its way to becoming a new moon), it is the time for rituals of banishment.

Chapter Six

The Tools of Wicca

Wiccans have a number of tools they use during their rituals. Traditionally, these objects were simple kitchen tools. Throughout time, they evolved into more ornate, and strictly ceremonial, objects. The tools are used for many different purposes, including purification of space, casting the circle, and magick work.

Tools of Wicca can be found in various places. Some are bought at New Age stores while others can be found at flea markets, garage sales, or antique shops. There is no right or wrong place to acquire ceremonial objects. It is believed that a tool will find you and you will know it is right for you because it will feel comfortable. Something else to remember is that tools are collected over a period of time. Acquiring your Wicca tools isn't like making a shopping list and getting all of your items at once.

Once the necessary items are collected, they need to be consecrated or blessed by the God and Goddess. This involves cleaning each piece and then performing a short ritual. There are a number of ways to "clean" an object, but the easiest way is with items found in most households. Once the object is cleaned, it is buried in salt or sand for a few days so that its old energies will leave. Another method calls for Wiccans to fill a tub with water and throw in a pinch of salt. Then the object is put in the water and left in there for a number of days. When the object is dug up or taken from the water, it is considered blessed.

The following objects are some of the more popular tools Wiccans use. Most are traditional and have been used since the ancient times. It isn't necessary to own every item on the list. And over time, you learn what works best for you.

The Athame

This is a dull, double-edged knife or dagger. It is used to direct energy during a ritual. Wiccans point with it or draw a pentagram into the air. The handle is usually dark and some Wiccans carve symbols onto it to personalize it. This tool is masculine and is linked to the God and the east.

The Bell

The bell is used to create music and rhythms. In Wicca, the bell is used to invoke the Goddess. It is

Spells, rituals, and other information can be passed from one generation of Wiccans to the next through the Book of Shadows.

believed that the sound of the bell sends out a magical vibration. The bell can also be used to ward off negative energies and evil spirits.

The Book of Shadows

The Book of Shadows is a book that contains beliefs, rules, rituals, spells, and any information that a Wiccan would want to write down and keep. Sometimes a Book of Shadows is passed down from generation to generation. The Book of Shadows is used for a number of things. A Wiccan can use it as a reference during a ritual. It can be used to write down feelings and thoughts much like a journal. Or, it can contain a list of herbs and favorite oils.

Covens like to make their own book and give copies of it to members when they are initiated. A misconception of the Book of Shadows is that there is only one version (like the Bible) that was created at the beginning of time and secretly passed on throughout the years. This is not true. There is no one book. Each Book of Shadows is just a compilation of what its creators choose to put in it.

The Broom

This tool is a symbol of protection. The broom is used to symbolically sweep the space and air around the altar to cleanse it. This makes the area sacred and ready for the ritual. The broom can be made from any

Flying Away

In ancient times, Wiccans would gather in the fields late at night with broomsticks. They danced to evoke energy that they believed would make the crops grow. As they danced, they would jump into the air to show the crops how high they should grow. Other people who saw them do this reported it to the king. The king was told that witnesses saw people flying around the fields on their broomsticks. Thus, the myth that witches fly on broomsticks was created.

type of wood, but favorites include ash, birch, and willow. The broom is linked to both the God and Goddess and is associated with the element of air.

The Cauldron

Most Wiccans have a cauldron that they keep either on, or close to, their altar. The cauldron is traditionally a large black pot that has three legs. It represents bounty and blessings. A cauldron is used in various ways. Wiccans cook herbs, boil liquids, and burn incense in their cauldrons. They also use cauldrons to cleanse spells. The cauldron is linked to the Goddess and associated with the element of water.

The Censer

The censer is an incense burner. There are many kinds to choose from including ones that hang. Using the censer to burn incense cleans the air around the space much like the sweeping with the broom. Also like the broom, it is associated with the element of air.

The Chalice

This is a special cup that is used during all rituals. Wiccans ceremonially drink from it during libation (the time when they give "thanks"). By taking a sip from the cup or by pouring a portion of one's own drink into it, and then passing it around the circle for others to share, Wiccans create a bond between each other. The chalice is usually personalized with symbols. It is linked to the Goddess and associated with the element of water.

The Pentagram

The pentagram is a symbol widely used by practitioners of magick. It is a universal symbol of life. The pentagram is a five-point star enclosed in a circle. Each point has significance. The top point represents the spirit, which symbolizes the divine. The top left-hand point represents the element air, which stands for intelligence. The top right-hand point represents the element water, which stands for the emotions. The bottom

Spirit

Air

Water

Earth

Fire

left-hand point represents the element earth, which stands for the physical and for personal endurance. The bottom right-hand point represents the element fire, which symbolizes courage. The star is enclosed in a circle. The circle represents unity and is said to symbolize the presence of the God and Goddess.

This symbol is important because it is an instrument of protection. Wiccans wear the pentagram as a symbol of their religion.

When drawn on a piece of paper, sewn on fabric, or made as a plate, the pentagram becomes a pentacle. The pentacle is used on most altars to offer protection before the start of a ritual. If the ritual involves blessing an object, it is placed on the pentacle.

A major misconception many people have is that the pentagram represents evil and is the symbol of Satanists. It is true that Satanists do use this symbol, but they reverse the pentagram so that the spirit points downward. Unfortunately, most people do not bother to notice whether a pentagram is right-side up or upside down, and it is often mistakenly assumed to be a symbol of evil.

The Wand

The wand is a tool that has many uses and has been around for thousands of years. Wiccans use it to cast the circle, call the four corners, draw symbols in the air, or direct energy (much like they do with the athame). This tool is most important before the start of a ritual or gathering. Some use their wand to stir the liquids in their cauldron. The wand represents the God and is associated with the element of air.

There is a specific length to the wand that most Wiccans use. It is said to be the distance from your elbow to the tip of your forefinger. There are favorite woods that the wand should be made from. They include oak, elder, and willow.

A reverend high priestess of Wicca holds a ritual drum, which is played to raise energy in a circle of religious celebration.

These tools are generally used when one begins to practice Wicca. Some Wiccans stop using them once they feel more confident in their ability to follow their intuition. Those who stop feel that the tools are props. Others feel more complete without them. Most, however, never stop using the tools. They feel that the tools not only aid them, but are part of the ornamental aspect of the ritual.

Chapter Seven

Divination and Meditation

Besides the spiritual aspects of Wicca, there are other practices associated with the religion. One example is divination, which is the ability to tell the future. You may wonder, can this really be done? Well, no one has ever been able to prove that they know the future. But there have been many people who seem to have an amazing ability to see what the future holds. And they are said to receive this information through visions. Nostradamus was one such individual—many of the things he predicted actually happened. Some events even occurred hundreds of years after his death. Aside from visions, there are many tools that can be used to predict what is to come or help one make the best decisions for a happy future.

- ◆ Tarot. Tarot is believed to have been around since the thirteenth century. To practice tarot,

Many people believe that tarot card readings can provide information about one's past or future.

one uses a deck of tarot cards. There are seventy-eight cards per deck and each one has its own meaning. By spreading the cards out in various ways, psychics or readers are able to tell someone about events that have happened and events that may happen in the future. The deck is split into two sections called the major and minor arcana. The most common spread that is used in a reading is called the Celtic cross.

• Runes. Runes are a system of symbols used in magick. Each rune has its own meaning. Some examples are victory, love, possession, and fertility. Runes come from the ancient Norse. The word "rune" means "secret" or "tree." The tree was a sacred symbol to the Norse because it represented where we come from (its branches are the above), who we are (its trunk), and where we go (the roots). The symbols are believed by some Wiccans to have come from the Goddess and represent properties of a tree. There are thirty-three runes in all, and they branch out from five properties: knowledge, healing, life, spirituality, and personality. Like tarot, combinations of runes give people insight into the future and help them to make good choices.

• Astrology. Astrology is based on a map of the sky. The map is made according to the locations of the sun, moon, stars, and planets at a particular time. Each person's sky pattern, or map, is unique and depends on where and when he or she was born. A year is broken down into twelve astrological signs called the zodiac. They include Aries, Taurus, Gemini, Cancer, Leo, Virgo, Libra, Scorpio, Sagittarius, Capricorn, Aquarius, and Pisces. Throughout the ages, astrologers have created meanings and symbols

Astrology is an ancient practice, based upon the movements of planets and stars.

for each of the zodiac symbols. When you combine your pattern with the given definitions, it gives you a description of your personality, how you react to certain situations, and what the future will hold for you.

◆ Numerology. Numerology also deals with patterns. It is the science of decoding numbers to reveal their hidden meaning and symbolism in your life. For example, the combination of the numbers associated with your name, and those in your date of birth can give you an idea of what the future will hold in terms of love, career, and health.

- Tea leaves. Reading tea leaves is known as tasseography. In tea reading, you drink the tea and the leaves that remain in the bottom of the cup, which form patterns, are read. They may form the shape of a letter, heart, or a ring. There are some standard symbols that are compared to each pattern. It is believed that psychics can use the leaf patterns at the bottom of a cup to make a prediction about the person whose future they are reading.
- Palmistry. This is the art of reading a person's palm. It began when our ancestors would sit around and tell stories. Because hand gestures were an important part of communication, a fascination developed with the hand. Everyone is said to have their own unique set of lines and patterns on their palms. Each line and pattern reveals something about that person. Readers are able to predict future events and tell a person about his or her personality by "reading" these lines.

Meditation

Meditation is the act of quieting the mind. It is a way to escape from the concerns of the day and gives a person the opportunity to let his or her mind and body relax. During this quiet time, a person can reflect on issues in his or her life. Wiccans use meditation to open their minds. Oftentimes, they attempt to focus their subconscious minds on being aware of any messages that may be sent to them from the God and Goddess.

How Do You Meditate?

Start out in a sitting position, preferably cross-legged. Sitting is the most comfortable position and many prefer it to lying down. With your back straight, chin level to the floor, eyes closed, and hands resting on your knees, begin to take deep breaths.

Take a deep breath and slowly release it. Repeat this breathing and feel your body start to relax. Forget your troubles. Never mind the list of errands you have to run tomorrow. Meditation is about being in the present and allowing yourself to relax.

Meditation Journal

Once you have started meditating on a regular basis, you may want to keep a journal of your experiences. What thoughts came to you? Were there any significant messages? How did you feel during the experience? These are just some of the questions you can ask yourself. Your journal may start to give you insight into parts of yourself about which you were not aware.

A Final Word

Wicca is a peaceful, nature-loving religion that is often misunderstood. Wiccans are not unapproachable or

Wiccan Teen Wins Case

On March 22, 1999, practicing Wiccan and student Crystal Seifferly won her case against Michigan's Lincoln Park school board, whom she had taken to court because they banned her from wearing a pentagram. Because the pentagram is a symbol of her religion, the school district was ordered to change its policy and also pay her legal fees.

evil, Satan-worshiping individuals. They are normal human beings who work and live in much the same way as everyone else. For example, teenage Wiccans have to study for their exams just like their peers.

Wiccans understand that not all people can and will understand their religion and methods of practice. But as long as they are able to practice according to their beliefs, they encourage others to do the same.

Glossary

Artemis   The Greek moon goddess, often portrayed as a virgin huntress.

athame   A dull double-edged knife used in rituals.

Book of Shadows   A journal-like book of rituals and spells that can be used by an individual Wiccan or shared in a coven.

coven   A group that meets during sabbats and other times and practices Wicca.

divination   The art of telling the future by using tools (like tarot cards and runes) and having visions (psychic power).

equinox   Two days of the year, usually around March 21 and September 23, when the sun crosses the equator and day and night are of equal length.

initiation   Admission into a group or religion.

karma The energy that is created from every emotion, thought, or action a person commits throughout his or her life.

magick The movement of energy for a purpose.

meditation Quiet time taken to reflect on one's life and quiet one's mind. Wiccans use meditation to receive messages from beyond.

reincarnation The process of being reborn into a new body.

ritual A ceremony used to produce a desired effect.

runes System of symbols used in magick.

sabbat A Wiccan holiday. Examples include Beltane, Imbolc, Lughnasadh, Mabon, Midsummer, Ostara, Samhain, and Yule.

solstice The two days of the year, around June 22 and December 22, when the sun is furthest from the equator. The December day is the shortest day of the year and the day in June is the longest day of the year in the northern hemisphere.

Wicca A religion of nature.

witch One who practices witchcraft or Wicca.

witchcraft The practice of the craft—using energy combined with herbs, stones, colors, and objects of nature to create a desired result.

For More Information

Web Sites

Covenant of the Goddess
http://www.cog.org
This site has a section, entitled Next Generation, that provides teens with useful information.

Fabrisia's Boschetto
http://fabrisia.com
This site contains information on Strega, an Italian form of witchcraft.

Spirit Online
http://www.spiritonline.com
This site contains information on different religions and on spirituality. It has an in-depth section on Wicca and a great dictionary of Wiccan terms.

Welcome to Wicca
http://www.members.tripod.com/leedouglas
This is a personal Web site that contains a lot of useful information about Wicca.

The Wiccan Church of Canada
http://www.wcc.on.ca
This organization has three different temples located throughout Canada where one can take classes and worship.

The Witches' Voice
http://www.witchvox.com
This organization's Web site contains everything there is to know about Wicca. Teens can search its databases and find contacts, stores, events, and organizations around the world. It also discusses Wicca in the media and other related current events.

Witch's Brew
http://www.witchs-brew.com
This site contains a teen e-mail list. Teens can discuss the craft with other teens once they subscribe.

For Further Reading

Cabot, Laurie, and Tom Cowan. *Power of the Witch: The Earth, the Moon, and the Magical Path to Enlightenment.* New York: Delacorte Press, 1998.

Cabot, Laurie, and Jean Mills. *The Witch in Every Woman: Reawakening the Magical Nature of the Feminine to Heal, Protect, Create, and Empower.* New York: Delta, 1998.

O'Hara, Gwydion. *Pagan Ways: Finding Your Spirituality in Nature.* Saint Paul, MN: Llewellyn Publications, 1997.

RavenWolf, Silver. *Teen Witch: Wicca for a New Generation.* Saint Paul, MN: Llewellyn Publications, 1998.

Starhawk. *The Spiral Dance: A Rebirth of the Ancient Religion of the Great Goddess.* San Francisco: Harper San Francisco, 1999.

Valiente, Doreen, and Evan Jones. *Witchcraft: A Tradition Renewed.* Custer, WA: Phoenix Publishing, 1990.

Index

About the Author

Geraldine Giordano is a Leo who is interested in tarot, astrology, and the occult.

Special Thanks

To Adriana Skura and Meg Green for all of their support and insight.

Photo Credits

Cover by Adriana Skura. All interior photos by Adriana Skura except p. 8 © Carl Vanderscuit/FPG International; pp. 11, 50, 57 © AP/Worldwide; pp. 13, 19, 23 © Corbis; p. 17 © VCG/FPG International.

Layout

Geraldine Giordano